RUSSIA

WORLD ADVENTURES

BY HARRIET BRUNDLE

KidHaven
PUBLISHING

Published in 2019 by
KidHaven Publishing, an Imprint of Greenhaven Publishing, LLC
353 3rd Avenue, Suite 255, New York, NY 10010

Designer: Matt Rumbelow
Editor: Charlie Ogden
Writer: Harriet Brundle

Cataloging-in-Publication Data

Names: Brundle, Harriet.
Title: Russia / Harriet Brundle.
Description: New York : KidHaven Publishing, 2019. | Series: World adventures | Includes index.
Identifiers: ISBN 9781534526167 (pbk.) | 9781534526150 (library bound) | ISBN 9781534526174 (6 pack) | ISBN 9781534526181 (ebook)
Subjects: LCSH: Russia (Federation)–Juvenile literature. | Russia–Juvenile literature. | Soviet Union–Juvenile literature.
Classification: LCC DK510.23 B77 2019 | DDC 947–dc23

Printed in the United States of America

CPSIA compliance information: Batch # BS18KL: For further information contact Greenhaven Publishing LLC,
New York, New York at 1-844-317-7404.

CONTENTS

Page 4   Where Is Russia?

Page 6   Weather and Landscape

Page 8   Clothing

Page 10   Religion

Page 12   Food

Page 14   At School

Page 16   At Home

Page 18   Families

Page 20   Sports

Page 22   Fun Facts

Page 24   Glossary and Index

Words in **red** can be found in the glossary on page 24.

WHERE IS RUSSIA?

Russia is the largest country in the world. Russia is spread across the continents of Asia and Europe.

RUSSIA

EUROPE

ASIA

MOSCOW, RUSSIA

The **population** of Russia is over 143 million people. The capital city of Russia is called Moscow.

WEATHER AND LANDSCAPE

During the winter, the weather in Russia can be extremely cold and there is often snow. In the summer, the weather is usually warmer, but is still very cold in many places.

Russia is so large that it has a wide range of different landscapes, including grassy plains and mountains.

CLOTHING

A sarafan is a **traditional** style of dress worn by women in Russia. A sarafan can be patterned or plain.

People in Russia usually wear comfortable and **modern** clothing.

RELIGION

The religion with the most followers in Russia is Christianity. Other people follow religions such as Islam.

A Christian place of **worship** is called a church.

FOOD

Pelmeni is a popular dish in Russia. It is a type of **dumpling** and is usually filled with meat.

PELMENI!

Soup is also popular. Shchi is a type of cabbage soup that is often eaten in Russia.

SHCHI

AT SCHOOL

Children in Russia start school when they are six years old and finish when they are seventeen.

ты говори́шь
по-ру́сски?

At school, children study subjects such as the Russian language, **politics**, and science.

AT HOME

An izba is a traditional style of house in Russia. These houses are made from wooden logs.

Most people in Russia live in large towns or cities. They usually live in houses or apartments.

FAMILIES

Family is very important in Russia. Most children see their grandparents, aunts, uncles, and cousins very often.

In Russia, it is **polite** to offer visitors to your house a treat, such as a sweet biscuit.

Tula gingerbread is a traditional Russian treat.

HOCKEY
STICK

The **national** sport of Russia is called bandy, which is also known as Russian hockey. Bandy is played on ice.

Some other popular sports in Russia include basketball, soccer, and gymnastics.

GYMNASTS

FUN FACTS

1. Mount Elbrus is the highest mountain in Russia and is over 3 miles (4.8 km) high.

Forests in Russia are home to animals such as reindeer, wolves, and bears.

2.

3. The computer game Tetris was invented in Russia by a man called Alexey Pajitnov.

4. Over 100 languages are spoken in Russia.

GLOSSARY

dumpling   a small ball of dough, often filled with meat

modern   something from present or recent times

national   relating to, characteristic of, or common to a nation

polite   being respectful of other people

politics   the decisions or actions of the government of a country

population   number of people living in a place

traditional   related to very old behaviors or beliefs

worship   a religious act such as praying

INDEX

children 14–15, 18

Christianity 10–11

clothing 8–9

families 18

food 12–13, 19

houses 16–17, 19

Islam 10

schools 14–15

sports 20–21

Photocredits: Abbreviations: l-left, r-right, b-bottom, t-top, c-center, m-middle.

Front Cover – Alexander Pekour, bg – Aleksey Klints. 1 – Aleksey Klints. 2 – Reidl. 3 – Alexander Pekour. 5 – Baturina Yuliya. 6 – LeniKovaleva. 7 – YURY TARANIK. 8 – Ruslan Iefremov. 9 – Iakov Filimonov. 10 – Igor Bukhlin. 11 – dimbar76. 12 – Anna Mandrikyan. 12 – Anna Mandrikyan. 13 – Lesya Dolyuk. 14 – Poznyakov. 15 – nito. 16 – Andrey Demkin. 17 – Sergei Butorin. 18 – Iakov Filimonov. 19 – Sann von Mai. 20 – Pukhov Konstantin. 21 – Lilyana Vynogradova. 22tl – Vasily Deyneka. 22br – Fufachew Ivan Andreevich. 23tl – Radachynskyi Serhii. 23br – Lucian Milasan. Images are courtesy of Shutterstock.com. With thanks to Getty Images, Thinkstock Photo and iStockphoto.